BEASTS &
BEHEMOTHS

DUNGEONS & DRAGONS®

BEASTS & BEHEMOTHS

A Young Adventurer's Guide

WRITTEN BY JIM ZUB

WITH STACY KING AND ANDREW WHEELER

TEN SPEED PRESS
California | New York

CONTENTS

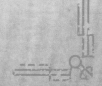

INTRODUCTION

Beasts are intriguing. Behemoths are terrifying. Both can make a story surprising and memorable.

This book takes you on a tour of some of the tiniest and tallest monsters from the world of DUNGEONS & DRAGONS. It will tell you where they come from, how they act, and advise you on overcoming their dangers.

Read this guide from start to finish, or open it up at any spot, see a cool illustration that catches your eye, and begin your journey from there. The more you read, the easier it will be to craft your own stories of sweeping adventure against the minuscule and the mighty.

Will your quests lead you to conquer colossal creatures, creating a legacy spoken of for generations, or will you be destroyed, fallen and forgotten? In the end, the decision is yours. DUNGEONS & DRAGONS is all about building new stories, and yours can begin right now.

Enjoy!

DANGER LEVELS

Each monster profile includes a number indicating the danger level of that creature, with a **0** being harmless, a **1** as a reasonable threat for a beginning adventurer, and building up from there. A **5** is incredibly dangerous and requires an experienced group of adventurers to possibly defeat it. There are some **epic** creatures more powerful than a mere number can define. Such terrors can only be fought by legendary heroes armed with the most powerful magic weapons and spells imaginable.

TINY & SMALL

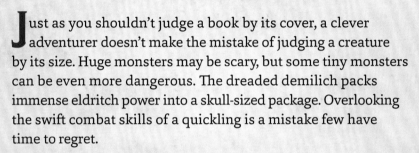

Just as you shouldn't judge a book by its cover, a clever adventurer doesn't make the mistake of judging a creature by its size. Huge monsters may be scary, but some tiny monsters can be even more dangerous. The dreaded demilich packs immense eldritch power into a skull-sized package. Overlooking the swift combat skills of a quickling is a mistake few have time to regret.

Tiny and small monsters pose unique challenges. Their size can make them harder to hit with weapons or spells. They're also prone to working in large groups, which can rapidly overwhelm their targets. One cranium rat is an irritation. One hundred are a serious problem. Are you ready to catch some critters?

CRANIUM RATS

O-1

SWARM POWERS A swarm of cranium rats can communicate telepathically, and thinks of itself as a single, unified creature. These swarms have limited psychic powers, which act similarly to spells, allowing them to understand languages, detect thoughts, create confusion, and issue simple commands.

SIZE Cranium rats are about as big as a sneaker, ranging from toddler-sized ones to the massive shoes worn by professional basketball players. A swarm of cranium rats is composed of up to three hundred individual rats. Swarms are just what they sound like, huge groups of rats that run together in unison as a furry wave of chittering destruction. A swarm of cranium rats is capable of fully engulfing an adult human.

Adventurers expect to encounter rats as they journey through ruins, dungeons, and underground lairs. What they don't expect are rats with glowing, exposed brains and keen telepathic powers. These unnatural creatures are made when normal rats are bombarded with the psychic power of a mind flayer (read more about these telepathic terrors in *Monsters & Creatures*). The elder brains that rule over mind flayer colonies use these augmented rodents as spies, infiltrating surface settlements and transmitting back all that they see and hear to their nefarious underground masters.

A single cranium rat is only as smart and dangerous as a normal rat. However, when united in a swarm, the rats become telepathically linked, increasing their intelligence and their danger level. Whether alone or in a swarm, cranium rats are protected by a cerebral shroud that blocks all attempts to read their thoughts and sense their emotions. They can also cast a dim glow around themselves using the light emanating from their pulsing little brains.

LAIR Cranium rats are most often found underground, in or around the lairs of mind flayers. While on a spying mission in a humanoid settlement, they can be found resting in the same spots as normal rats, including barns, sewers, and other small, dark places.

DO THIS

Watch for their glow. Cranium rats give off a dim light that is easily spotted in dark places.

Keep them separated. Individual cranium rats are much less dangerous than a swarm.

DON'T DO THIS

Don't keep one trapped. If the mind flayer elder brain is within range, it can see and hear anything that happens around the cranium rat. Making plans in front of a telepathic spy is a really bad idea.

DEMILICH

5

ARCANE ABILITIES Although demiliches can no longer cast spells, they still have many magical powers. Their bloodcurdling howl can frighten and even kill opponents. They can drain the life force of nearby creatures, using this energy to heal their own injuries, and they can swirl up their dusty remains to blind enemies. They are immune to many types of damage, such as poison and psychic attacks, and are even resistant to magical weapons.

SIZE A demilich is a bejeweled skull the size and shape of whatever creature it once was in life. Most are small enough to be held in two adult human hands, although touching one is not a good idea.

Attempting to cheat death itself, a great wizard may pursue vile rituals to bind their soul to a magical object called a phylactery, which transforms the wizard into an undead creature called a lich. They must sacrifice souls to the phylactery on a regular basis to maintain their physical form. If they fail to do so, their bones turn to dust, leaving behind only a skull.

A demilich, as this creature is called, can no longer cast the powerful spells it once knew, yet remains a deadly foe. Their lairs are complex crypts guarded by monsters and traps. Within these vile vaults, the demilich calls upon arcane powers that allow it to summon earthquakes, block magical attacks, and prevent healing. So long as its phylactery exists, the demilich cannot be completely destroyed, for its form will regrow after several days. Worse still, if the demilich succeeds in feeding even a single soul to its phylactery, its body will revive from the dust—and along with it, all the lich's magical might!

LAIR A demilich resides within a labyrinthine tomb protected by monsters, traps, and magical wards. Its skull and the dust of its bones will often be found within, at the tomb's most secure spot, along with the demilich's treasures and its carefully hidden phylactery.

DO THIS

Destroy its phylactery. This magical object most often takes the form of a small box or amulet with silver sigils inside. Finding and destroying this artifact is the only way to stop a demilich once and for all.

DON'T DO THIS

Don't use Turn Undead. This cleric power can ward off normal undead creatures, but demiliches are immune.

Don't plug your ears. The fiendish howl of a demilich can't be stopped by physical barriers.

LEGENDARY DEMILICH
ACERERAK

SIZE Acererak's form is an adult-sized skull decorated with precious magical gemstones. His eye socket gems are the size of golf balls, while the ones replacing his teeth are each as big as a fingertip.

Becoming a demilich is not always a bitter end for a lich. When made as a conscious choice, it can be the next step in a dark evolution, freeing the spellcaster from the last restrictions of their physical form while retaining a spark of their original self. Acererak is one of the few who has succeeded in harnessing this transformation for their own evil ends.

A powerful wizard and occult explorer, Acererak abandoned his physical form to travel through other planes of existence. He collects arcane artifacts and locks them away in trap-laden tombs. These elaborate dungeons are intended to lure powerful adventurers with the promise of great rewards. Most often, these heroes wind up failing in horrible ways, thanks to the devious devices and malicious monsters they encounter. Acererak then traps their souls in his phylactery, fueling his magical power.

Acererak's legend has inspired others to follow a similar path, though not always with success. The demilich has little interest in apprentices. His focus is on taunting the adventurers who dare enter his violent vaults. In time, he intends to evolve further, into an even more powerful and terrifying archlich form. Whether he will be successful in this dark endeavor remains to be seen.

LAIR Acererak has many lairs scattered across the physical plane and beyond. Each one contains great treasure and also great danger. The most famous of these is the Tomb of Annihilation, a deep complex constructed on the isle of Chult. The location of Acererak's true lair, which hides his precious phylactery, remains a mystery.

SOUL GEMS Anticipating the collapse of his body, Acererak set enchanted gemstones into the eye sockets and teeth of his own skull. These gems can capture the souls of his opponents, trapping them inside the glittering stones. Victims of the soul gems can be freed only by destroying the gems within twenty-four hours of capture. Otherwise, the trapped soul is devoured by Acererak's phylactery and ceases to exist.

PSEUDODRAGON

DRACONIC FAMILIARS Some pseudodragons are willing to bond with a spellcaster, becoming what is called a familiar. This bond allows the spellcaster to share the pseudodragon's magical resistance when they are nearby (within ten feet) and to communicate telepathically for up to one mile. However, pseudodragons retain their free will while bonded. They will not hesitate to break this connection and leave a companion who treats them poorly.

SIZE Pseudodragons are about the size of a large parrot and weigh slightly less than a house cat. They're small enough to sit on your shoulder, if you don't mind risking a few scratches from their sharp claws.

Imagine a terrifying dragon shrunk down to the size of a teddy bear. That's a pseudodragon. With red-brown scales, leathery wings, and ridged horns, these diminutive beasts can frighten adventurers who mistake them for their larger, more terrifying cousins.

Despite their small size, pseudodragons are far from helpless. Their thick scales help them resist magic, while their keen senses make them hard to sneak up on. When attacked, pseudodragons defend themselves with sharp teeth and an even sharper stinger, which delivers a poison that can knock out opponents for up to one hour.

Pseudodragons possess a limited form of telepathy that allows them to communicate simple ideas, images, and emotions to language-using creatures within one hundred feet of them. In addition, they often vocalize their moods with animal noises, purring to indicate happiness or hissing in surprise. These playful creatures are highly prized as companions, especially by magic wielders.

LAIR Pseudodragons prefer to live in quiet, isolated places. They can be found in the hollows of trees and in small caves, or in the quiet nooks of a spellcaster's library.

DO THIS	DON'T DO THIS
Offer friendship. These picky creatures can sometimes be won over with gifts of food or treasure.	**Don't rely on magic.** A pseudodragon's scaly hide gives them resistance to spells and other magical effects.
Listen for the unsaid. They may try to communicate with you using emotions or images, so stay alert for telepathic messages.	**Don't take them for granted.** If you are lucky enough to bond with a pseudodragon, be sure to treat it right. They will quickly abandon anyone who manipulates or abuses them.

PSEUDODRAGON

Florizan Blank was hoping to track down the hobgoblin tribe that raided Red Larch, but he wasn't a ranger and the trail he'd followed this far seemed to have run its course. The bard knelt to look closer at the patches of dirt and trees nearby, to see if he could spot more footprints, and that's when something else caught his eye—dusky crimson scales, glittering dark eyes, and bat-like wings stretching out before him. It was a dragon . . . with a body no bigger than his backpack?

"Hello there, friend," Florizan said, laying on a bit of his legendary bardic charm. "Are these your woods I wander through?"

The pseudodragon tilted its head inquisitively, chirping out a cautious reply. Florizan could feel a thrum of curiosity emanating from the tiny beast. Cautiously, he pulled out the last of his dried meat rations. The creature was too wary to take it from his hand, so Florizan tossed the food in the air, laughing as the pseudodragon spun to catch the morsel mid-flight.

"Clever and charming!" he exclaimed. "No wonder wizards are so fascinated by your kind."

An idea flashed in Florizan's mind. Spellcasters prized pseudodragons, and he needed a favor from one—a way to remove a curse from his friend who was bitten by a werewolf a few weeks ago. Florizan had no guarantee he could tame this creature, however, and the attempt would disrupt his search for the hobgoblins. Even if he did succeed, would he be able to give up such a delightful companion?

What should Florizan do next? If he tries to tame the pseudodragon, will his bardic spells and kindness do the trick? What happens if he accidentally angers the pseudodragon and it attacks? Will neglecting his search for hobgoblin tracks leave Red Larch vulnerable to another raid? The choice is up to you!

QUICKLING

BLURRED MOVEMENT Quicklings move so fast that they appear blurred to most other creatures, which makes them very hard to hit. Their remarkable dexterity makes them resistant to spells and other attacks that affect speed. While not invisible, their indistinct form is hard to observe. An adventurer needs to be very alert and perceptive to spot a quickling, even one that's rifling through your backpack for treasure.

SIZE Quicklings are about as tall as a greyhound and just as skinny—not that most of them will stay still long enough to be measured.

Once upon a time, there lived a race of lazy, selfish fairy creatures. Eventually their idle ways offended a dark fairy queen and she cursed them with smaller size and a rapid sense of time.

To quickling eyes, the mortal world moves at a dreadfully slow pace. Raindrops fall like drifting feathers, lightning inches across the sky, and other creatures might as well be standing still. In turn, quicklings appear to most creatures as hazy blurs, often accompanied by high-pitched rapid laughter. They can only be seen and heard when they deliberately slow down, a process that is excruciating for the impatient quicklings.

Quicklings delight in pranking slower creatures, using their speed to move objects and create mischief. Sometimes these pranks are relatively harmless, but they can be serious, such as hiding important documents or framing an innocent person with stolen goods. Quicklings delight in ruining other people's lives, perhaps because their own are so short—at their sped-up pace, quicklings burn through their lives in just fifteen short years.

LAIR Quicklings favor haunted, twisted forests where dark creatures thrive. They can be found in both the mortal realms and the fairy lands, known as the Feywild.

DO THIS

Catch them as fast as you can. A quickling tied up or otherwise restrained cannot move fast enough to remain blurry, making them much easier to deal with.

Protect your shins. Quicklings may use tiny daggers, but they can strike three times to each one of yours. Those rapid little cuts can take down even the strongest adventurer.

DON'T DO THIS

Don't ignore odd events. Shoelaces suddenly tied together? Rations gone when you turn your back? There could be a quickling nearby!

Don't trust their advice. Quicklings are mischievous creatures. If they slow down enough to speak with you, it's probably to set up one of their nasty pranks.

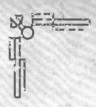

MEDIUM

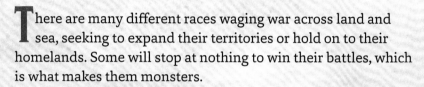

There are many different races waging war across land and sea, seeking to expand their territories or hold on to their homelands. Some will stop at nothing to win their battles, which is what makes them monsters.

From hobgoblin armies to sahuagin raiding parties, medium-sized monstrosities are often at their most fearsome when they strike as a group. A raiding party of orcs can seize a village in a single day, while a handful of drow can plunder a town in a single night. That said, there are deadly individuals at this size also. It might only take one death knight to raise an army from the ruins of a battlefield—and a medusa always acts alone, though they're often surrounded by a parade of statues, victims of their cursed gaze.

Read on and you'll meet creatures your adventurers can face eye to eye. Just be warned that they might not be so happy to see you!

ANIMATED ARMOR

FALSE APPEARANCE When motionless, animated armor looks just like a normal set of armor. There's no way to tell unless you use a detect magic spell or get close enough to wake it up.

SIZE Any suit of plate mail can be transformed into animated armor. Most are around six feet tall, the usual size of human plate mail. Using plate mail designed for halflings or gnomes results in animated armor about three feet tall, while an especially powerful creator might enchant a suit of giant-sized armor, producing an animated servant that stands ten feet or more in height.

Brought to life by potent magic, animated armor obeys the commands of its creator, so long as these orders are clear and uncomplicated. Some are able to speak simple phrases, allowing them to warn intruders, demand a password, or deliver riddles. Encountering an eerie voice booming out of an empty helmet is enough to rattle even the bravest adventurer!

Animated armor is almost always constructed from plate mail, which is durable but heavy. The metal crashes together as the armor moves, clanging loudly with every step. Animated armor makes for a useful guard, since it requires no food, rest, or even air. Some activate only when intruders are close, while others may be set to follow a regular patrol along a fixed path. Once it attacks, animated armor will not stop until it is too badly damaged to keep moving—which means, unfortunately, that it's also too damaged to be salvaged as armor by adventurers after the battle is finished.

LAIR Animated armor exists only within the lair of its creator, often a powerful spellcaster. As such, they can be found in castles, crumbling manors, ancient temples, dusty dungeons, and other places inhabited by those with a lot of magic and at least a little treasure to protect.

DO THIS

Approach abandoned armor with caution. You never know when that plate mail propped up against the wall or lying on the ground might spring to life.

Use antimagic spells. Animated armor is brought to life by magic, so using an antimagic field or a dispel magic spell can render it immobile for up to one minute.

DON'T DO THIS

Don't try to have a conversation. Even when animated armor can speak, it will only know a few set phrases. You won't get far asking it for information.

Don't think they're alive. Animated armor is immune to attacks that affect living creatures, such as poison, psychic attacks, and spells that blind, frighten, or charm.

DEATH KNIGHT

4

SPECIAL POWERS

HELLFIRE ORBS

Hellfire orbs provide death knights with their most devastating attack. These balls of flame burn everyone caught in their explosion and leave any survivors' skin rotting like a corpse. Thankfully, death knights can only use this deadly attack once a day.

MARSHAL UNDEAD

Death knights can command nearby undead creatures and strengthen them against divine magic.

SIZE Like paladins, death knights can come from any race, which means that they can be various sizes, ranging from small goblins to imposing dragonborn. Their imposing armor adds to their bulk, making them even scarier on the battlefield.

Paladins are noble knights who fight in service to their gods and harness divine power in battle—but even these paragons sometimes fall from the path of the righteous. When a paladin offends their god and fails to make amends for it before they die, they can be brought back from the grave by dark and terrible forces as a death knight!

Death knights wield formidable magic power in service to the new masters that resurrected them and they can cast powerful spells, though they have none of the healing magic paladins often use when alive. Death knights' most fearsome gift may be their ability to command the undead, allowing them to raise entire armies of shambling corpses to do their bidding! Some even revive skeletal beasts that they ride into battle.

Death knights are challenging enemies because they cannot be laid to rest until they make peace with the god they offended. Until that time, they will rise again after each defeat.

LAIR Death knights wander freely, with no need for a permanent home, provisions, or comforts. You might find one close to where it fell in life, near a temple of the god it failed, or on a battlefield where it hopes to raise the dead as its minions.

DO THIS

Keep a cleric handy. Clerics are very useful when battling the undead, since many have a divine gift which lets them repel or even destroy such creatures.

Learn the knight's story. If you can identify the death knight and learn why it was transformed, you may be able to persuade it to atone for its mistakes and leave its undead existence behind.

DON'T DO THIS

Don't expect to kill a death knight. It can't be done! Your best hope is to get away as far and as fast as you can.

Don't die with unfinished business. If you're a paladin and you don't want to come back as a terrible monster, make sure you follow your god's instructions very closely.

LEGENDARY DEATH KNIGHT
LORD SOTH

SIZE Lord Soth is an imposing figure in his plate mail armor. In life, he stood six feet, five inches tall, and his armor stands a little taller. It's unclear how much of the undead man remains beneath the tarnished metal.

Lord Soth was once one of the Knights of the Rose, an order of elite fighters devoted to honorable combat. Jealousy and paranoia drew Soth away from the righteous path of his god Paladine, and he betrayed those he claimed to love, bringing destruction down upon them and himself. He might have sought redemption for his past, but a great cataclysm struck and he was consumed by fire.

Reawakened as a death knight, Soth now deeply resents the living and spends his restless undeath in service to dark forces that would see the whole world burn. He carries out his evil missions with intense focus and ruthless efficiency. However, in death, Soth has also rediscovered the honor that escaped him in life. He observes the rules of knightly conduct on the battlefield, which means he never strikes an unprepared opponent and never cheats to win. Even still, in combat he is a fearless opponent who will not hesitate to destroy a foe he deems worthy of his attention, and he will hunt down anyone who dares interfere with his plans.

LAIR Lord Soth's stronghold is Dargaard Keep, high on a cliff overlooking the surrounding lands. The keep was laid out in the shape of a rose, an ancient symbol of the knighthood, and its walls built from rose-colored stone, but any beauty it once held was lost long ago. Now it is home to terrifying undead creatures, while an aura of decay clings to the walls that have since turned black with corruption.

SKELETON ARMY Lord Soth's most loyal attendants in life were given new purpose in death, reawakened as skeleton warriors. Animated by dark magic, these mute soldiers follow their lord's word with total obedience, as their existence has no other purpose. Fighting against Soth on his own is already a terrifying prospect, but facing him and his fearless undead army at the same time would make almost any warrior's blood run cold with fear.

DROW

1

SPECIAL POWERS

DARK WEAPONS
Drow weapons, forged of a tough black metal named adamantine, are often coated with spider venom or infused with magic, though those enchantments fade if exposed too long to sunlight.

DEMON SUMMONING
All drow have magical abilities, but priestesses and wizards can sometimes call on demonic creatures to serve them.

SIZE Most elves are a similar height to humans, but being small is an advantage in the tunnels of the Underdark. Drow are often a little shorter than other elves, and the males tend to be slightly shorter than the females.

The Underdark is a vast network of tunnels, far beneath our feet, where many strange and dangerous races thrive. The most sophisticated of these races are the drow, an offshoot of the elves who were sent into exile below ground many centuries ago.

The drow built a new elvish society in the dark, living in service to the only god who did not abandon them: Lolth, the great Spider Queen of the Abyss. Under the many eyes of Lolth, the drow founded an Underdark empire. Matriarchs govern the elite drow families that dominate their society, and priestesses wield impressive magic power.

Drow rarely venture to the surface. Though they did not choose the darkness, they prefer it now, as sunlight hurts their eyes and limits their magical abilities. They still harbor a great hatred for other elven races, and sometimes venture above ground at night to attack other elves or to abduct people as slaves.

LAIR If you expect to find only simple mines, tunnels, and caves in the Underdark, the drow will surprise you. They've carved entire cities out of rock, as beautiful and vast as any aboveground elvish city. Non-drow are forbidden to enter, and these cities are defended by high walls and giant spiders.

DO THIS

Work with the sun. Their underground existence makes drow highly sensitive to sunlight. You'll have an edge if you can bring daylight, either natural or magical, into the fight.

Be smarter than they expect. Drow are raised to believe that surface-dwellers are inferior, which makes them vulnerable to clever traps and plans.

DON'T DO THIS

Don't go out alone at night! If you're near a drow city, keep the doors locked and stay inside at night, because that's when drow raids happen.

Don't wander into their cities. Only drow and their beasts are permitted to enter their cities in the Underdark. If any non-drow pass the city walls, they are usually killed on sight.

GNOLL

RAMPAGE ABILITY Gnolls can fight at a distance using longbows and spears, but their most dangerous attacks are up close, where they combine weapon strikes with a powerful bite. If a gnoll manages to badly injure an opponent up close, they can enter a temporary frenzy which allows them to follow up with a rapid chomp, inflicting even more damage.

SIZE Gnolls are the same size as an adult human, if that person had terrible posture and hyena legs that bent in non-human ways. Their elongated arms hang down past their knees.

Gnolls are feral scavengers who lurk on the boundaries of civilized lands, constantly seeking their next fight. These humanoid hyenas don't understand goodness or compassion, only mindless destruction. Everything they have is stolen from their fallen victims, including gruesome trophies like ears, teeth, and scalps, which they use to decorate their patchwork armor. Most horrifying of all is their habit of devouring their victims, leaving behind gnawed corpses among the burnt and ruined remains of once-peaceful homes.

Working together under the leadership of a pack lord, gnolls attack at random before vanishing back into the wilderness. They choose easy targets, ignoring fortified castles or walled cities in favor of vulnerable farms and poorly defended villages. Their victories are celebrated with foul rituals, blood sacrifices, and often more fights, for their destructive desires are never fully satisfied.

LAIR Gnolls rarely build permanent structures, instead taking shelter in forest thickets, caves, and other natural hiding spots. Their nomadic quest for new victims means they rarely stay in one place for very long.

DO THIS

Intimidate them. Gnolls avoid fighting powerful opponents, so you might manage to scare them off with a powerful display of strength or magic.

Stay back. Ranged weapons and spells will help you avoid their vicious claws and teeth.

DON'T DO THIS

Don't break up your group. Gnolls will use pack tactics to surround and overwhelm individual adventurers, so stick together.

Don't reason with them. They simply won't listen.

HOBGOBLIN

MILITARY EXCELLENCE

Hobgoblins have no special powers that are unique to their race. However, years of training and fighting make them some of the finest soldiers in the world. They're not just superb fighters, they also excel at other military tasks, such as setting and building traps, spying on enemies, and crafting weapons.

SIZE Hobgoblins are about the same size and height as humans. They are much bigger than their goblin cousins, but smaller than their bugbear cousins.

Goblins are small, cowardly creatures, known for their malice and mischief; but their warlike cousins, the hobgoblins, are a very different type of threat. Hobgoblins would sooner die than back down from a fight. These warriors are trained from childhood to be soldiers, raised in a culture of military discipline. They aspire to a valiant death in battle, making them fearless opponents.

One of the most reliable ways to break a hobgoblin's focus is to distract them with an elf. The hatred between hobgoblins and elves goes back centuries, and hobgoblins will often forget any other target if they see an elf in battle.

The toughest hobgoblins rise to the level of warlord, and they maintain their power with an iron grip. The legions under their control may include other creatures such as orcs, bugbears, and even goblins.

LAIR Hobgoblins live in strongholds that resemble army encampments, because everyone in hobgoblin society is part of the military, complete with military rank. Hobgoblins are always trying to expand their territory, building strongholds in any land they claim. Their homes are always well defended with obstacles and traps.

DO THIS	DON'T DO THIS
Show strength. Hobgoblins respect strength and valor.	**Don't be an elf.** If you are an elf, you'll be the first one the hobgoblins attack!
Think like a soldier. Hobgoblins approach everything with militaristic precision, which means a smart strategist might anticipate their plans.	**Don't mix up the goblin cousins.** Goblin culture and hobgoblin culture are very different, and hobgoblins consider themselves vastly superior to their smaller kin.

MEDUSA

1

PETRIFYING GAZE The gaze of a medusa can turn a person to stone in an instant—a process known as *petrification*—but sometimes the transformation happens slowly enough that a lucky adventurer has time to seek help. Only very powerful healing magic can reverse the effects of a medusa's gaze.

SIZE Most medusas are cursed humans or members of other human-like races, so they're the same size they were in their original form, though their hair may be a lot bigger!

Immortality and ageless beauty have lured many people to make deals with dark forces without fully understanding the dangers involved. When powerful wishes are granted, powerful curses are often attached.

Medusas are humanoids who have won the gift of eternal youth, but found that it comes at a terrible price. The corruption they embody manifests as living, writhing snakes in place of hair on their heads, and anyone whose eyes connect with those of a medusa will soon be turned to stone. This is the great irony of the medusa's curse; they will always be beautiful, but no one will ever see them again.

Because medusas are immortal and doomed to always be alone, they spend centuries slowly going mad in the confines of their grand homes. Their only entertainment is the destruction of anyone who dares disturb them.

LAIR Cut off from the world by their curse, medusas live in palaces, temples, and grand gardens that speak to the power and status they once enjoyed, but that slowly fall into disrepair and ruin. You might know you're in a medusa's lair if there are a lot of strange statues and no other people around. Medusas' lairs are often full of treasures, but only the foolish or very brave would seek them out.

DO THIS

Carry a mirror. If you can trick a medusa into staring at its own reflection, it will turn itself to stone. For this reason, you won't find any mirrors in a medusa's lair.

Carry a powerful healing potion. Only a potion of great restoration—or a spellcaster who can cast the same magic—can undo the effect of the medusa's gaze.

DON'T DO THIS

Don't risk a look. The easiest way to avoid a medusa's gaze is to never go anywhere near one. If you don't have a choice, find a way to navigate the medusa's lair with your eyes covered.

Don't seek out immortality. As many medusas will attest, living forever never ends well.

MEDUSA

Galeg had a plan when she came to Kingdom's Fall, the crumbling palace of an ancient and formidable medusa. She knew the treasure here was enough to buy her people back from the drow mines—but avoiding the deadly glare of the snake-haired Princess Amira would require stealth, cunning, and magic! Galeg put together a team and made sure every one of them carried a Stone Salve ointment that could revert the medusa's spell.

Then Amira attacked in the gloom of the catacombs, and the well-crafted team fled in all directions.

Now Galeg was alone, or so she thought. She crossed paths with another adventurer, a rogue from distant lands—and a moment later the medusa struck again.

Galeg stayed hidden, but the rogue was not so lucky. She could hear the young woman's cries as the petrification magic began to take hold. Galeg's plans had fallen apart. If Galeg saved this rogue's life, perhaps she could be a useful ally?

What should Galeg do next? If she saves the life of the stranger, she'll be vulnerable to the medusa's attack, and she has no guarantee that the rogue will even be able to help. But if she stays hidden, the rogue may die and Galeg will be all alone. It's up to you!

ORC

ELVISH HATRED All orcs share a deep loathing for elves, which traces back to their creation myths. During the early days of the world, Gruumish, who created the orcish race, was partially blinded by an elven god's arrow. Since then, orcs have taken a special delight in slaying elves in retribution. Elite orcs known as the Orc Eye of Gruumish go so far as to cut out one of their own eyes, believing that mighty Gruumish will grant them extra power in return for their offering.

SIZE Orcs are the size of a professional football player wearing all of their protective gear, and are heavy enough to break kitchen chairs if they sit down too quickly.

Orcs are savage marauders with an unquenchable drive for conquest and violence. They gather in tribes under the leadership of a war chief, who holds that role only while he can control the others with his personal strength and supply them with new targets for their anger. This patriarchal society sees strength and power as the highest virtues, and they welcome ogres, trolls, half-orcs, and even evil giants into their ranks.

Orcs are known by their stooped posture, gray skin, and prominent lower canine teeth, which resemble tusks. They wear hide armor and favor greataxes, javelins, and spears, which extend their already-long reach. Permanent orc settlements are rare, because once an area has been depleted of food and wealth, the tribe becomes restless and eager to move on to fresh battles. Many a village has counted themselves fortunate to survive an orc raid, only to learn that hunting party was merely scouting ahead for a vast horde of roaring warriors bent on blood and destruction.

LAIR Orcs make their homes in ruins, caverns, and the homes of their recently defeated foes. The common thread among all orcish lairs is the presence of crude defenses. Most lairs have sharpened sticks thrust into walls, moats surrounding them, and body parts of fallen enemies displayed as grotesque decorations.

DO THIS

Disarm them. Orcs are highly adept with their chosen weapons, which let them inflict extra damage in a fight, so take away that advantage if you can.

Watch for missing eyes. One-eyed orcs are often extra-strong; some may even be able to cast spells.

DON'T DO THIS

Don't target the war chief. Orcs operate as a tribal horde, not an army, so killing their leader won't cause them to flee.

Don't negotiate. Orcs think of truces as foolish words and will break them at the first opportunity.

SAHUAGIN

1

SPECIAL POWERS

ELVISH SPIES
Some mutated sahuagins, known as malenti, look so much like aquatic elves that they act as spies in their enemies' camps.

BLOOD FRENZY
The smell of blood in the water can make sahuagin more dangerous against wounded enemies.

SIZE Sahuagin are about the size of a professional middleweight boxer, although the larger four-armed types are closer to a heavyweight class. They all have thick necks, broad tails, and flexible fins on their forearms.

If the idea of swimming with sharks makes you nervous, that's nothing compared to the terror of swimming with sahuagin. These terrifying aquatic predators are as bloodthirsty as sharks, are twice as deadly, and can follow you onto the land.

Nicknamed sea devils, these underwater warriors are noted for their slashing claws and fearsome teeth. The largest and scariest, sahuagin barons, have four arms instead of two. As expert hunters, they often carry ranged weapons like spears or tridents. Their raids sometimes bring them to the shore to attack coastal towns and camps; but they can only survive out of the water for a few hours.

Sahuagin feel a close kinship with sharks, and worship a shark god named Sekolah. They can communicate telepathically with the creatures, training these sharks to attack their foes or even to serve as steeds in battle. Their greatest enemies are aquatic elves, whom they have battled for centuries to control the oceans.

LAIR As far as sahuagin are concerned, the entire ocean is their territory, and anyone else in the water is trespassing. They make their homes in the deepest, darkest trenches they can find. So, stay out of the dark water!

DO THIS

Listen. The wail of a conch horn signals a sahuagin hunt. If you ever hear it, chances are high that everyone around you has already started running!

Stay inland. You'll never meet a sahuagin far from the water, though they can chase you ashore if needed.

DON'T DO THIS

Don't spill blood in the water. Sahuagin can smell it (and so can sharks!).

Don't get caught between sahuagin and aquatic elves. The battles between these two ancient enemies are intense.

TROLL

LOATHSOME LIMBS Because of their weird regenerative powers, a troll can sometimes retain control of an arm or leg—or even its head—when it's removed from the troll's body, at least until it reattaches the body part or grows a replacement. That means you could be cut by a severed troll arm or bitten by a severed troll head.

SIZE Trolls are taller than humans, growing up to nine feet in height, which is taller than the tallest human that ever lived. They can appear smaller when they walk hunched on all fours.

Trolls are nightmarish creatures, not just because their greed for food and treasure makes them so unpredictable and violent, and not just because their sickly smell and ugly appearance make them terrifying, but because they have the strange ability to recover from almost any attack.

Trolls' long claws and deadly teeth are dangerous enough, but their rubbery bodies have remarkable healing powers. Squish a troll, and it will pop back up. Shoot it with arrows, and it will pull them out. Cut it to pieces, and it will try to put itself back together. Even lopping off its head won't kill it; a troll might just grow a new one! Only flames or acid can permanently harm a troll.

Sometimes trolls don't heal quite right, which only makes them scarier. An injured troll might accidentally grow a second arm, or even a second head. Some trolls also take on magical traits from other races—by eating them.

LAIR You may have heard that trolls live under bridges or in other dank, dark spaces. The truth is, trolls don't care where they live. They'll go wherever they can find food or things to smash, and they'll stay anywhere the locals don't chase them away.

DO THIS

Burn them. Acid and fire are the only attacks that can stop a troll from regenerating.

Look out for lopped-off limbs. Having a detached arm attack you from behind is an embarrassing way to lose a fight.

DON'T DO THIS

Don't think you can beat a troll with a sword. However successful you are in chopping up a troll, it always comes back and can attack again.

Don't try to hide. Trolls have an exceptional sense of smell.

YUAN-TI

1

SERPENT POWERS

Yuan-ti malison and abominations can transform fully into snakes that are the same size as their yuan-ti forms. All yuan-ti can communicate with snakes, enchanting them to do their bidding. Those with snake fangs can use their bite to pierce and poison foes, while those with tails can grapple opponents with this appendage, squeezing the life out of them.

SIZE Pureblood and malison yuan-ti come in the same range of sizes as humans, but yuan-ti abominations have long powerful tails that can make them twice as large from snout to tip.

As remorseless as the snakes they revere, the yuan-ti were once ordinary humans. Years of devotion to serpent gods transformed them, inside and out. Physically, they took on snake traits such as yellow eyes, venomous fangs, or scaled skin. Mentally, they turned cold and cruel, which empowered them to sweep across the land, establishing a vast and powerful empire. That empire has long since crumbled, but the yuan-ti still live in the ruins of their once great cities, plotting their return to glory.

Some yuan-ti still look almost human, with serpentine features that give them away. Called purebloods, these are the lowest ranking class of yuan-ti society. Above them are the malison, the hunter class, who may possess a snake's head, a snake's tail, or snakes instead of arms. Most highly revered are the rulers of the yuan-ti, giant serpents with humanoid torsos and arms, who are called abominations.

LAIR The great cities of the once mighty yuan-ti empire still exist in remote jungles and deserts, as ruins of their former glory. These cities are full of splendor and treasure—but every step may be watched by dozens of serpent eyes.

DO THIS

Look for yuan-ti carvings. If you're ever exploring ancient ruins, look for any signs of serpent worship. If it's a yuan-ti city, it probably hasn't been abandoned.

Watch out for purebloods. Pureblood yuan-ti will sometimes move among cities acting as spies, but their serpentine skin, eyes, teeth, or tongue may give them away.

DON'T DO THIS

Don't reveal your emotions. Yuan-ti see emotion as a weakness and will exploit any vulnerability you show. If they know who you care about, they may try to hurt that person to get to you.

Don't trust a snake. Any snake you meet could be the companion of a yuan-ti agent.

LYCANTHROPES

Lycanthropy is one of the most ancient and feared of all curses, transforming the afflicted humanoid into a ravenous beast. Despite this, it is also the easiest curse to hide. Its victims retain their natural form most of the time, although they may manifest hints of their cursed condition, like fur tufts or pointed ears, which can be spotted by keen observers. Only when the lycanthrope chooses—or is compelled by the power of a full moon—does their inner animal surface, unleashing a savage frenzy.

A lycanthrope can either defy its curse or embrace it. Resisters retain their original morals but cannot fully bond with their beastly nature. When the transformation strikes, they lose all control and may not even remember their rampages. Those who embrace their fate learn to master their shape-changing abilities. The downside is the replacement of their mortal values with dangerous, animalistic instincts.

Lycanthropes can appear in three different forms: their original humanoid shape, a powerful version of a normal animal, and a hybrid physique which combines aspects of both, typically an upright, humanoid body topped with an animal's head.

REMOVING THE CURSE

There are two ways to acquire lycanthropy: either by being wounded by a lycanthrope or by being born to a parent who carries the curse. In the first case, a Remove Curse spell cast by a cleric, paladin, wizard, or warlock can restore the victim. For lycanthropes born into the curse, they can only be freed by the magic of a powerful Wish spell.

WEREBEAR

SIZE Werebears are tall and broad-shouldered by the standards of their humanoid race. In beast form, they are as large as a full-sized adult bear and stand on all fours unless attacking with their claws. Their hybrid form towers over even the tallest human.

Of all lycanthropes, werebears are the most able to control their monstrous impulses. They are solitary creatures, unwilling to risk accidentally passing along their curse. New werebears are typically either born to the condition or carefully chosen after a period of apprenticeship. Great care is taken to help them adjust to the curse, ensuring that they learn to accept and control their powers.

In humanoid form, werebears are large, muscular people with dense hair that matches the color of their fur in beast shape. Their hybrid and animal forms are even larger, featuring thick fur and sharp claws. Although their teeth are powerful weapons, they avoid using them whenever possible, relying on their greataxes and claws instead. Werebears turn their curse to good use by protecting the flora and fauna of their chosen territory from intruders.

LAIR Werebears may reside in either woodland cottages or natural caves, depending on whether they wish to be known as a humanoid or a bear to their neighbors. Most live in a landscape that matches their bear form to reduce the risk of their curse being discovered.

WEAPON IMMUNITY Like all lycanthropes, werebears cannot be hurt by normal weapons, although they can be damaged by magical ones. Silver is the only metal capable of wounding a lycanthrope. Some well-prepared adventurers will take the precaution of having their weapons plated with silver, but this is expensive and requires an expert blacksmith.

DO THIS	DON'T DO THIS
Negotiate. Werebears are the most rational of lycanthropes and may listen to reason if approached respectfully.	**Don't trample the flowers.** Werebears do not tolerate reckless damage of plants or trees under their care.
Keep your distance. Werebears have an immense reach and can claw targets up to five feet away from them.	**Don't overstay your welcome.** You don't want to be around if a werebear loses control.

WEREBOAR

SIZE The beast form of a wereboar can be as large and heavy as a riding lawn mower. They are just as big in hybrid shape. Their humanoid shape tends to be short and squat compared to others of their race, and their hair takes on a rigid, wiry texture.

Perhaps the grumpiest of all lycanthropes, wereboars are reckless about infecting others with their curse. In both their boar and hybrid form, they can gore targets with their massive tusks, potentially passing along their curse with each wound inflicted. They take satisfaction in watching their victims struggle with the savage changes wrought by the curse.

These ill-tempered and rude brutes live in small family groups in remote forest areas. They are quite suspicious of strangers, but sometimes ally with orcs. Their humanoid forms are stocky and strong, with short, stiff hair. Their hybrid shape is covered in the same stiff hair, combined with a snarling boar's head. Their tusks are their preferred weapon, but they can also use other weapons while in humanoid or hybrid form.

LAIR Wereboars are content with relatively primitive shelters, taking refuge in caves or constructing ramshackle huts. Most settlements are small, with only one or two families. Not even other wereboars can put up with their crankiness for long!

RELENTLESS Wereboars are powerful fighters capable of taking remarkable amounts of damage and continuing to fight. When a wereboar is hit with a blow that would knock most other creatures unconscious, their stubborn nature and toughness helps them stay on their feet. In addition, their beast and hybrid forms can charge a nearby target, knocking their victim to the ground.

DO THIS	DON'T DO THIS
Avoid their tusks. Unlike many lycanthropes, wereboars are eager to pass along their curse.	**Don't use normal weapons.** Like all lycanthropes, wereboars can only be damaged by silvered weapons or magical attacks.
Stay upright. Wereboars will try to knock you over, making it easier for them to gore and trample you.	**Don't mind their manners.** Wereboars are inherently rude, so don't take it personally.

WERERAT

1

RAT ATTACKS Wererats are quick and agile. They can squeeze their giant rat bodies into surprisingly small spaces, letting them escape even when seemingly cornered. They have a keen sense of smell that lets them track prey through crowded spaces and over great distances. Their speed also lets them make multiple attacks in rapid succession, and they don't hesitate to bite targets, even though doing so risks passing along their curse.

SIZE The hybrid form of a wererat is not much larger than their humanoid size, and it varies depending on their original race. In giant rat form, they are about as tall as a two-year-old child and take up as much space as a coffee table.

Wererats are sly, greedy shapeshifters known for their cunning nature. They favor ambush, stealth, and secrecy over open conflict. In human form, wererats are wiry and flighty, with thin hair and beady, twitchy eyes. Their hybrid form combines the head of a rat with thin, lightly furred limbs and sharp claws. As a beast, they become giant-sized rats, several feet tall with sharp teeth and a long, leathery tail. They prefer to fight in human or hybrid form, wielding light weapons such as shortswords, daggers, and hand crossbows. Their rat shape is typically reserved for spying or escape, although it can fight back viciously if cornered.

Wererat clans operate much like thieves' guilds, with their own code of conduct and clearly defined territory. They treat the curse as a clan induction, only sharing it with selected humanoids. A wererat who tries to break away from their clan or who receives the curse through an accidental bite can expect to be ruthlessly hunted down by the other wererats of the same clan.

LAIR Wererats can be found in cities across the realms, creating their burrows in the sewer systems, cellars, and catacombs of urban centers. Rats of both normal and giant size often live alongside wererats, serving as spies, guards, and pets.

DO THIS

Pay for information. Wererats tend to be well-informed about the cities where they live and greedy enough to share that knowledge with adventurers, for a price.

Watch for ambushes. These stealthy creatures use strategy and shadows to overcome their foes.

DON'T DO THIS

Don't disrespect their turf. Wererats respond poorly to anyone who challenges their ownership of subterranean spaces.

Don't rely on normal weapons. You'll need magic or silvered items to do damage to a wererat.

WERERAT

"Ship's ready, then?" asked the wiry half-elf in a nervous voice.

"Aye," replied her human companion. "Pickup is midnight at Sorrel Beach."

Tinglym grinned from her hiding spot behind a large crate. The gnome ranger had been tracking this smuggling ring for weeks, hoping to recover what they'd stolen from Daleport. This was the lead she needed.

"Hang on. Somethin' smells like gnome," said the half-elf, lifting his nose in the air. Seconds later, the crate was thrown aside. "We've been made!"

To Tinglym's shock, the human began to change shape, his skin bristling all over with gray fur as his face elongated into a rat's sharp snout. "Run and warn the others. I'll take care of this sneaker."

Without a word, the half-elf transformed into a giant rat, whiskers twitching as she raced toward a crack in the cavern wall. Tinglym hadn't expected the smugglers to be lycanthropes, and she only had a moment to decide how to handle this strange revelation.

What should Tinglym do? If she fights the hybrid wererat, does his companion get away and warn the other smugglers, changing the plan and allowing them to escape with their stolen loot? If she tries to stop the escaping wererat, can she avoid being clawed in the back by its ally? Or should she run away from both of them and come back later with reinforcements? The choice is yours!

WERETIGER

POUNCE Like a housecat with a toy, weretigers can pounce on their targets from at least fifteen feet away, delivering a powerful claw strike that can push an enemy off their feet. Weretigers' keen hearing and sense of smell allow them to track victims from a distance, and they have an advantage when their pounce is a surprise.

SIZE In their humanoid form, weretigers tend to be taller and leaner than typical members of their race. Their beast shape is as big as a dining room table.

Sleek, elegant, and deadly, weretigers reflect both the refined and ferocious sides of their feline nature. They tend to be taller than average for their humanoid race, growing even larger in their beast and hybrid forms. Despite this size advantage, weretigers prefer to fight in their humanoid form, since it reduces the risk of accidentally passing on their curse. They favor the curved blade of the scimitar in combat, as it suits their fluid fighting style, and they rely on longbows for targeting enemies at a distance.

These territorial creatures like to keep their distance from civilization, living alone or in small family groups. While they do not mourn their curse, they are reluctant to increase their numbers, since each new weretiger is a potential rival for hunting grounds and prey. They are meticulous about their grooming and always cut a graceful form. Their hybrid shape is covered with sleek, striped fur, while their tiger form stands twice as tall—or more—than most humans.

LAIR Weretigers gravitate toward jungle landscapes, although some may be pushed toward less desirable terrain by strong rivals. They adapt to the environment, setting up shelter within caves, treetops, and other suitable spots.

DO THIS

Approach with respect. Weretigers are open to interacting with others, so long as those interactions are polite.

Fight close. A weretiger's pounce only works from a distance, so staying close will keep you from being knocked off your feet.

DON'T DO THIS

Don't make a mess. Weretigers like things clean and neat. Creating clutter is sure to irritate them.

Don't let them change forms. Weretigers might not like to fight in hybrid or animal form, but they will when desperate.

WEREWOLF

SHAPESHIFTING Like all lycanthropes, werewolves who have given in to their feral instincts can learn to control their powers and change shape at will. Those who hold on to their humanity are at the mercy of their curse, transforming during the peak nights of the full moon. In either case, lycanthropes return to their original form when killed. In some cases, this may be the first time an adventuring party realizes what they've been fighting against!

SIZE A werewolf's hybrid form is almost as tall as a regulation soccer net. Their humanoid form does not change much from their pre-cursed size, although they often become hairier.

Werewolves are savage predators with heightened senses that are relentless in tracking their chosen prey. After being cursed, they rarely remain in civilized lands for long, for the ferocity of their new instincts makes it difficult to stay hidden. Those who fight the curse live in dread of what they might do to family and friends, while those who embrace their condition fear the consequences of their bestial crimes.

Although a powerful fighter in both humanoid and wolf shapes, werewolves are at their most terrifying in hybrid form. The combination of a furred, muscular body with a wolf's head strikes a primal fear in even the most hardened of adventurers. Although werewolves can wield weapons in their human and hybrid forms, they prefer to use claws and teeth to rip apart their victims, a mark of their savage instincts taking control.

LAIR Werewolves live in wild places, carving out territory in tangled forests, windswept hills, and snowy mountains far from humanoid settlements. They tend to move around their domain frequently, sleeping in the open or in narrow caves depending on what is available.

DO THIS

Heed the full moon. This is the night you're most likely to encounter an out-of-control werewolf.

Invest in silvered weapons. They'll be crucial if you encounter a lycanthrope of any kind.

DON'T DO THIS

Don't let them bite you. Being a werewolf might sound cool, but living with a curse is really no fun.

Don't assume new moon nights are safe. Werewolves who have embraced their curse can be dangerous at any time, even on moonless nights.

LARGE & HUGE

Part of what makes a hero is the willingness to face monsters that are bigger than you—in some cases, way, *way* bigger. Keeping your nerve in the face of a towering ogre or slavering dire wolf is no easy feat.

In some cases, bulk is the only advantage these creatures possess, and a clever adventurer can get the upper hand with some quick thinking. Don't assume every big creature you encounter has sacrificed brains for brawn! Inscrutable sphinxes and mysterious minotaurs present complex challenges that even the smartest hero will find challenging, not to mention the danger posed by the insectile intelligence of the umber hulk.

Massive and mighty monsters await you in the following pages. Are you ready to encounter adventure when it comes supersized?

CORPSE FLOWER

SIZE Corpse flowers are big enough to bust out of a backyard greenhouse, if you were unfortunate enough to have one growing inside.

Corpse flowers sprout over the remains of evil necromancers or powerful undead creatures, taking root in the tainted dirt. Left undisturbed, these seedlings will grow to an enormous size in just a few weeks before tearing loose from the earth using powerful, ropy tentacles. And that's when things get really bad.

These wicked weeds scavenge humanoid corpses from battlefields and graveyards, stuffing the bodies into their fibrous form. If bodies cannot be found, these villainous vines are willing to make some fresh ones, for they are driven by a hatred of all living creatures. A fully grown corpse flower can hold up to nine bodies, digesting them as needed to repair itself. These bodies can also be reanimated and spit out as mindless zombies, which act to protect the plant until they are destroyed or dispelled by magic.

LAIR Corpse flowers can only take root where powerful undead magic has been destroyed. Once grown large enough to move, they are drawn to cemeteries and combat zones where they can find bodies to harvest.

STENCH OF DEATH Corpse flowers give off a powerful stench that causes nausea and temporary immobility to anyone within a ten-foot radius. Creatures who manage to guard themselves from the smell, or are immune to poisons, can avoid these effects, but the dangerous odor sticks around for two to eight days after the corpse flower is killed.

DO THIS	DON'T DO THIS
Notice that smell. Their distinctive stench makes it hard for corpse flowers to sneak up on people.	**Don't get complacent.** Corpse flowers can climb difficult surfaces and even travel along ceilings, so watch in all directions.
Avoid the tentacles. They hit hard and can even poison you.	**Don't ignore strange sprouts.** Uprooting a corpse flower at the seedling stage is much easier than fighting a fully grown one later.

DIRE WOLF

1

TAMING A DIRE WOLF Goblins, orcs, and other such evil creatures prize dire wolves as pets, guards, and even mounts, but taming one is no easy task. The best method is to capture one as a pup and raise it by hand with plentiful treats, but even that is no guarantee of success. Obtaining a dire wolf companion is a long and difficult process requiring patience, animal handling skills, and a dash of luck.

SIZE Dire wolves are slightly larger than a hippopotamus, but much faster (and furrier!).

Picture a wolf that's twice as big as you, with glimmering eyes and thick fur in mottled gray or black. Now picture it snarling at you while it decides which morsel to eat first. That's a dire wolf.

These huge beasts are fierce pack hunters who use stealth to surround targets before striking in unison. Their enormous jaws are capable of mighty bites that can tear an opponent off a horse, and their keen senses make it easy for them to follow their prey, especially through their own territory.

Like their smaller cousins, dire wolves tend to live in packs. Solitary dire wolves do exist, although they are rare. Often, solo dire wolves will form a pack with normal wolves for shared protection and companionship.

LAIR Dire wolves favor hills and wooded areas with natural caves that can serve as a den for their family unit. Such lairs tend to be messy and primitive, scattered with gnawed bones and leaves as bedding.

DO THIS	DON'T DO THIS
Watch for tracks. Druids and rangers are especially skilled at spotting the signs of a nearby dire wolf.	**Don't threaten their pups.** Like most wild creatures, dire wolves are most dangerous when their young are at risk.
Keep your distance. Dire wolves can only attack nearby enemies, so stay back and target them with arrows, thrown weapons, and ranged spells.	**Don't ignore the pack.** Dire wolves are rarely alone, so keep watch for flanking attacks by other pack members.

GIRALLON

FLYING FISTS! The four giant arms of the girallon are not just for climbing and swinging. A girallon can attack you with all four of its fists in a single strike, and then attack with its bite as well. That's five attacks from the girallon in the time it might take you to fire a bow or cast a spell—and their claws and fangs are very sharp.

SIZE A gorilla on its hind legs can grow to about the same height as a human. Girallons are bigger—and heavier. Some weigh as much as half a ton.

Going toe-to-toe with a gorilla would be scary enough; imagine facing a giant white gorilla with four arms and razor-sharp claws on each hand!

Girallons are monstrous gorilla-like creatures with gray skin and white fur. According to legend, they may have been created by powerful spellcasters to guard their lairs. Some girallons are still used by other races as guards or workers. However, their wild nature makes them difficult to control, and most girallons now live in their own communities deep within tropical jungles.

Girallons live in large family groups. They hunt for food alone and in packs, and despite their large size, they're surprisingly cunning, with an exceptional sense of smell. You should hope you're never the prey in a girallon hunt, because these apelike beasts will be upon you before you even know what's happening.

LAIR Girallons would like to live high in the trees where they can look down on their surroundings, but they're too heavy! Most girallon tribes live on the ground or in caves, but sometimes they find abandoned human habitations and take them over. Ruined cities, temples, and palaces can be home to sprawling girallon communities, and the stone walls of those structures allow them to climb as high as they like.

DO THIS

Offer gifts. If you can earn the trust of a girallon pack leader, the group will not attack you.

Stay out of the ruins. Once girallons have claimed a fallen city or temple as their own, they will fiercely defend their territory.

DON'T DO THIS

Don't come in arm's reach. Those four arms can do a lot of damage!

Don't get caught up in the hunt. If girallons are on the scent of their prey and you get in the way, they may decide that you're a more interesting target.

MINOTAUR

SIZE Minotaurs can grow to as much as twice the height of the average human, though they sometimes slouch if the ceilings are low.

If you ever find yourself turning down endless corridors or pathways that seem to lead nowhere and you hear a snort of breath or a low rumble of hooves, get ready to run or fight. You're in a maze, and there's a minotaur nearby.

Minotaurs are huge, muscular creatures with giant horns and animal features that resemble a bull, though they can be any gender. The labyrinths they occupy serve as a sort of sacrificial temple to their dark god, the Horned King, who created the first minotaurs by transforming loyal followers into beastly monsters.

Minotaurs serve their master by spilling the blood of anyone foolish enough to enter their maze. They're fast and strong, and their first attack will often involve trampling you into the ground!

LAIR Minotaurs don't have to live in labyrinths, but they will if they're faithful servants of their god. Don't assume that all labyrinths look the same. Some are stone-walled corridors, but natural caves, forests of twisted trees, or the winding ruins of an abandoned palace can also be made into mazes by a minotaur.

LABYRINTHINE MEMORY Minotaurs can live their whole lives inside labyrinths, waiting for the unwary to step inside, and they are masters of the maze. They remember every turn and every path of their homes, and they always know exactly where they are. They also have excellent senses, so they know where *you* are too.

DO THIS	DON'T DO THIS
Dodge. You're probably a lot smaller than the minotaur, which can be an advantage when avoiding attacks.	**Don't go into a labyrinth.** The best way to avoid a minotaur is to never enter a maze.
Leave a trail. Markings or a long rope can help you find your way back out again. Just hope that no one messes with your trail.	**Don't get lost.** As soon as you get lost in a labyrinth, you're at the minotaur's mercy.

OGRE

ULTIMATE OMNIVORES Ogres are omnivores, which means they eat all kinds of food—but they also try to eat a lot of things we wouldn't consider food. They're not picky eaters. Their favorite things to eat are halflings, dwarves, and elves, and their version of fast food is an elf that tries to run away.

SIZE Ogres can grow up to ten feet tall and can weigh more than a large horse—especially if they've just eaten a large horse!

Ogres are famous for being as stupid as they are hungry, and ogres are very, very hungry. These large, lumbering creatures are too simple and lazy to farm, work, or make their own food, so they attack other people and eat their food instead. If those people don't have any food, they'll just eat the people.

Anything ogres can't eat, they may keep as treasure. They don't know the value of anything, but they take things that other people think are valuable, and they like gold because it shines. The only real culture ogres have is crafting things from leftovers, like bone jewelry and animal skin rags.

Ogres sometimes form ogre gangs that roam around causing trouble, or they join forces with other creatures like orcs and trolls, but they have no sense of community. The one exception is giants. Ogres think giants are the best, and giants think ogres are useful fools who can sometimes be used to perform simple tasks, like destroying a village or eating an enemy.

LAIR Ogres don't really have homes. They eat until they're tired, and then they fall asleep wherever they want. However, they like to be close to places where they might easily get another meal, like farms and villages. Sometimes they move into remote cabins and cottages, but they always eat the people living there first.

DO THIS

Distract them. Shiny objects will often draw an ogre's attention. Lead them away from you with a trail of coins or trinkets.

Hide. It's easy to set off an ogre's bad temper. Your best chance of surviving an encounter is to make sure they never see you at all.

DON'T DO THIS

Don't seem too smart. Ogres don't like being made to feel stupid. If they think you're trying to trick them, they will eat you.

Don't be too delicious. If you're a dwarf, elf, or halfling, you look a lot like dinner to an ogre.

ONI

SHAPECHANGING Oni can magically transform into a small or medium humanoid, into a large giant, or return to their true form in an instant. They retain the same strength, stamina, and spellcasting regardless of what they currently look like. Oni prefer to use a weapon called a *glaive*, a two-handed polearm which changes size to match their current form so they are never unarmed. If killed, both the oni and its weapon revert to their true sizes.

SIZE In their true form, oni are as tall as a playground swing set and weigh twice as much as a grand piano.

By day, oni appear as innocent travelers, using magic to hide their true form. They gain the trust of those they meet, all the while planning to betray their new friends. At night, they transform in both shape and size, becoming the boogeymen of nursery rhymes and nightmares. Stealth and cunning are their trademarks, and their favorite technique is to kidnap targets and drag them home for a future meal. These monstrous creatures are always hungry, and babies are their favorite delicacy.

With their black teeth and claws, blue-green skin, and short ivory horns, oni are a terrifying sight. Their true form is more than twice the size of normal humans, but they can magically shrink to be as small as a gnome. Their powers include the ability to create darkness, to become invisible, to turn into a gaseous form, and even to regenerate wounded flesh. They also have the power to charm people, allowing them to win the trust of wary targets. Oni covet magic and will serve evil spellcasters in exchange for magical items, a lavish lair, or other material rewards.

LAIR The cunning oni prefer to dwell in fortified structures or underground lairs. Some are willing to trade their service to an evil magic user in exchange for luxurious and well-defended quarters. They linger on the edges of civilization, never wanting to be too far from potential prey.

DO THIS

Tempt them. Oni crave magic, so showing off a magical item might cause them to accidentally reveal themselves.

Watch for unusual strength. If you're clever, you might trick an oni into using its full strength while in a smaller form.

DON'T DO THIS

Don't sleep easy. If someone new has joined your group, it's a good idea to have a rotating watch on them at night.

Don't let them escape. Oni are much harder to fight in their well-protected lairs.

SPHINX

2-4

SPECIAL POWERS

SPELLCASTING
Sphinxes can call on a wide range of powerful spells that grant them near total control of their surroundings. They can even teleport, making them tricky to fight.

CLAWS
Sphinxes can swipe an attacker with two mighty claws when magic isn't enough.

ROARS
Androsphinxes have a powerful roar that is terrifying the first time you hear it, paralyzing the second time, and like being struck by an ear-shattering sonic boom the third time.

SIZE Because they are shaped by their divine masters, sphinxes can be any size, and they may use illusions to disguise their form. However, they are typically about the length of eight regular cats—or two lions!

When a god wants to keep a secret, sphinxes are the ones they call on to protect it. These regal creatures, with lion bodies, eagle wings, and humanoid faces, are spirits or faithful servants of the gods that are granted form and power to protect divine treasures from thieves and adventurers alike.

Tireless in their watch, sphinxes don't just protect treasures; they determine who is worthy to receive any power those treasures may grant. An androsphinx (male sphinx) will set tests of valor for visitors to perform. A gynosphinx (female sphinx) is more likely to ask riddles. If you pass its test, the sphinx will allow you to continue your quest. If you fail, you will be sent away or destroyed.

Sphinxes have extraordinary power to bend time and reality around them, and they can use this power as part of their tests. A sphinx may transport you to another plane of reality in the blink of an eye to see how you survive there—or just make you think you've been transported, when you haven't actually moved at all.

LAIR As guardians of divine treasures, sphinxes live wherever they are needed, maintaining a constant vigil without food, water, or sleep. You may find them in remote temples, dungeons, or tombs. Powerful weapons or magical items they are guarding will surely be close by.

DO THIS

Try to pass their tests. Whatever riddles or tasks the sphinx sets for you, you're expected to do your best.

Be respectful. If you fail, the sphinx may choose to destroy you or simply to send you away, so be polite.

DON'T DO THIS

Don't try to read their minds. Sphinxes are immune to those forms of magic and will probably notice if you try anything tricky.

Don't sneak past. Sphinxes can see you even if you're invisible or disguised. Stopping you from getting past them is their one job, and they do it well.

SPHINX

"There is treachery among you."

The sphinx's words seemed to boom around the frozen cavern, yet Orvar knew he had only heard them in his mind.

"You and your friends came here seeking wisdom. Here it is. One of your group places greed above kindness, and that person will doom you all. I have frozen time for a moment so you may act. Choose the friend you think is most likely to betray you and place this poison on their lips.

"Choose wisely, and I will give you your reward. Defy me, and you will pay a terrible price."

Orvar stared with confusion at the icy-cold vial that had appeared in his hands and wondered what he should do. He and his party had traveled together for a year. They were more than friends; they had become a family. He could not believe any of them would hurt the others for any reason!

Yet he had to do something, and swiftly, or the sphinx would deliver a devastating punishment. Who would he choose? The weakest among them? The quietest? The loudest? The one he argued with the most? Or should he strike at the sphinx instead? He knew sphinxes were powerful, but perhaps he would get lucky?

The sphinx narrowed its eyes. It demanded an answer.

What would you do if you were Orvar and your fellow adventurers were your best friends? Would you attack the sphinx and risk destruction, or poison a member of your party? Is there another option that Orvar might try? It's up to you!

QUEEN LULUAH

5

SIZE Luluah was a young woman when she was transformed into a sphinx, and she is smaller than other sphinxes—about the size of a lioness. Other sphinxes like to appear grand and imposing, but Luluah wants her visitors to understand that great power sometimes comes in small packages.

Luluah was once the young queen of a mighty kingdom lost thousands of years ago. She had warned her council that a flood was coming and tried to organize her people to restore the plains and forests that might protect them, but the council ignored her warnings and removed her from the throne.

When the flood finally came, Luluah feared she would drown in the lavish chambers that had become her prison. Instead, the goddess Chauntea came to her with an offer. Luluah had served Chauntea faithfully, and her reward was to live on eternally as a sphinx.

Luluah now defends the treasures of Chauntea's divine garden. She uses her powers to inspire brave young women to answer the call to adventure, and she only admits visitors that include such a hero in their party. Her challenge is simple: Did the other members of the party listen to the women who travel with them, or did they ignore the women and speak over them? Only those who answer well may seek a gift from the great garden.

LAIR Luluah is the protector of a garden where plants of great magical power can be found. The garden exists outside of reality, but can be accessed through magical groves that are sacred to the goddess Chauntea.

PSYCHIC GIFTS Luluah is skilled at projecting her mind into the minds of others, even at great distances. She can read thoughts that people hope to keep buried, inspire thoughts in those who seek encouragement, and even use her gifts to see through the eyes of other cats. Sometimes she visits the minds of the women she inspires, to experience their adventures along with them!

UMBER HULK

CONFUSING GAZE The hypnotic powers of the umber hulk can strike anyone close enough to see its eyes. Anyone who falls under its magic gaze will be temporarily unable to move, or will move in a random direction, or sometimes even lash out wildly at the people around them, even if those people are their closest friends.

SIZE Umber hulks grow to about eight feet tall, which means their antennae would probably brush the ceiling of the rooms in your home.

Parents in the Underdark tell their children scary stories about the umber hulk. If you don't finish your dinner and do your chores, the umber hulk will get you.

There are a few reasons why these large bug-like creatures are so scary. First, they have deadly claws and mandibles for crushing their prey. Second, they have an armored hide made from a tough substance called chitin. Third, they want to eat you up!

More terrifying than any of that, however, are their eyes. The gaze of an umber hulk can scramble your mind. Umber hulks like to find a place to hide where they can jump out and surprise passing prey, and one glance can leave their victims stunned, unable to run away or even defend themselves.

People who have survived an umber hulk attack are often those who didn't see the creature at all, just the carnage it created. That's why people tell scary stories about the horrible monster that lurks in the dark that few people ever live to see.

LAIR Umber hulks nest in underground burrows, but you're more likely to find them lying in wait for unsuspecting passersby in nooks and crevices in the rocks—or, more accurately, they're more likely to find you.

DO THIS

Pay attention in the Underdark. Umber hulks lie in wait for their prey, so your best hope is to notice where they're hiding before they jump out at you.

Look away. You are safe from the umber hulk's gaze so long as you don't look at the creature.

DON'T DO THIS

Don't just look away. If you're not looking at the umber hulk, it will try to attack you with its claws and mandibles!

Don't hurt your friends. If your friends attack you because of an umber hulk encounter, remember it's not their fault. Try to disarm or contain them!

METALLIC DRAGONS

In worlds of fantasy, the most famous magical creatures are dragons. Many legendary dragons are chromatic—white, green, black, blue, and red. These winged reptiles covet treasure and destroy any who dare cross them.

But there are others as well, good-aligned dragons who do not seek out violence or destruction. Good dragons are metallic—brass, bronze, copper, silver, and gold. Each has different abilities and breath weapons. If you need assistance against powerful evil forces or knowledge of ancient treasures, understanding the differences between these dragons could change the course of your quest.

The size and power of a dragon depends on its age, which also determines its danger level. Wyrmlings are babies, younger than 5 years, who are as tall as a human and quite vulnerable. Young dragons are 6 to 100 years old and between eight and sixteen feet tall. An adult dragon is 101 to 800 years old and between sixteen and thirty-two feet tall. Ancient dragons are older than 800 years. These massive terrors are more than thirty-two feet tall, and some reach forty feet or larger.

All adult dragons can create huge gusts of wind with their wings or swing their large tails to knock over targets. Their powerful jaws can rend flesh and bone, and their sharp claws easily pierce non-magical armor. Older dragons generate a supernatural fear that can terrify opponents just by being near them. Most metallic dragons serve the forces of good, but that doesn't mean they're selfless or weak. These dragons are just as frightening as their chromatic relatives and should be approached with great caution.

BRASS DRAGON

3-5

SPECIAL POWERS

SLEEP BREATH

In addition to fire, brass dragons can switch their breath weapon to exhale a potent sleep gas that can knock out any who breathe it in. Targets who go unconscious this way won't wake up for ten minutes, unless someone else injures them or shakes them awake.

FIRE BREATH

A brass dragon can breathe scorching fire from deep within their bodies. The heat this generates can easily melt flesh and burn clothes or even armor.

Brass dragons are the most curious and conversational of all metallic dragons, but don't let that fool you into thinking they're any less dangerous than their brothers and sisters. Their inquisitive nature imparts a deep desire to acquire items and knowledge, and if they decide they're intrigued by you or your possessions, you may soon be their unwilling guest for a time while they ask some pointed questions!

LAIR Brass dragons crave hot and dry climates and they can typically be found in deserts, ruins, canyons, or caves with ceiling holes to allow sunlight to enter.

Brass dragons conceal their treasure hoards under huge mounds of sand or in secret places far from their lair. They know exactly where this treasure is buried, so don't expect to find any maps that lead the way. If you stumble across treasure that seems abandoned in the desert or locked in the far chambers of a ruin, be careful. Brass dragons can sometimes give gifts to people who give them new tidbits of knowledge or entertain them with deep conversation, but they do not take kindly to thieves.

DO THIS

Bring information. Brass dragons love to discover new things, and someone who engages them with fascinating material may be able to impress them.

Bring a gift. Brass dragons acquire treasures from their journeys and love items that have a story of their own. A good gift and an accompanying tale can go a long way to gaining their trust.

DON'T DO THIS

Don't try to trick them. Just because they're talkative doesn't mean they're gullible. Brass dragons are very smart and react poorly to those who try to manipulate them.

Don't cut conversation short. Brass dragons love to talk and they live a very long time, so they're rarely in a rush. If you're going to seek out a brass dragon, be prepared to give them your time and attention.

BRONZE DRAGON

3-5

SPECIAL POWERS

FIRE BREATH
Much like blue dragons, their sworn enemies, bronze dragons can breathe out bolts of lightning that scorch and blind their foes.

REPULSION BREATH
In addition to lightning, bronze dragons can exhale powerful repulsion energy. This force doesn't hurt the target, but it does intensely push back anything within its path.

Bronze dragons dwell on the coast and are fascinated by those who travel the waterways near their lairs. Some bronze dragons even shapechange into dolphins or seagulls to inspect ships and their crews.

These curious swimmers are infamous for their skills in looting sunken ships or finding rare pearls from deep seabeds located near their homes. Like many metallic dragons, they will take cursed or sinister items into their protection to keep them from falling into the hands of evil.

Bronze dragons are fascinated by warfare, and some join battles just to test their abilities against armored soldiers or siege weapons. The battles of humanoids are a bit of a game to them, as they know they will outlive any military force or dwelling they encounter.

LAIR Bronze dragons tend to claim coastal caves as their dens, though some have been known to use shipwrecks or even surfaced coral reefs as well.

DO THIS

Stay calm! Bronze dragons like to inspect travelers on the water. If you can keep your composure, they probably won't attack.

Give them military items. Bronze dragons are fascinated by the way humanoids gather and armor themselves for battle. If you have books on military history or ceremonial treasures from a great battle, you may be able to befriend them.

DON'T DO THIS

Don't gather your navy. Large fleets of ships and military operations at sea can attract the attention of bronze dragons.

Don't shortchange them. Bronze dragons can sometimes be convinced to help in exchange for treasure, but make sure the terms of this barter are clearly defined and pay exactly what you owe.

COPPER DRAGON

3-5

SPECIAL POWERS

ACID BREATH
Much like black dragons, their sworn enemies, copper dragons can breathe a spray of burning acid, scorching anyone unlucky enough to be hit by it.

SLOWING BREATH
In addition to acid, copper dragons can exhale powerful energy that magically slows everyone in its path, making their foes an easy target for any attack they choose.

Copper dragons are notorious pranksters who love telling jokes and riddles. They're quick with a laugh, but just as quick to demonstrate a jealous and possessive streak as well, making them hard to deal with and incredibly dangerous if they feel they're not being properly appreciated.

These bold and boisterous reptiles love to play tricks, but they don't always realize that what they think is funny may not be as amusing to the lesser creatures with whom they fool. A target of a copper dragon's mirth who doesn't respond with good humor can quickly become an enemy. With the power to crush buildings, breathe gouts of acid, and cast spells, copper dragons are certainly not a foe you want to face.

LAIR Copper dragons tend to dwell in dry uplands or hilltops where they usually make their homes in narrow caves. They're incredibly protective of their treasure, even more than other dragons, and rarely have their most prized items out for public display, preferring to keep them hidden in secret antechambers behind powerful protective spells or traps.

DO THIS

Bring them music and art. Copper dragons love music, poetry, and all forms of art. In fact, some have even become close friends with bards and made room for them to stay in their lairs so they can be regaled with stories and songs.

Have a good sense of humor. If a copper dragon plays a trick on you, it expects you to accept it and laugh. If not, then you may see how quick it is to shift to anger.

DON'T DO THIS

Don't get burned. Protect exposed flesh from nasty acid burns. Wear a heavy cloak, and be prepared to cover yourself if the creature unleashes its powerful breath attack.

Don't lose your patience. Copper dragons believe their time and attention is valuable to everyone they encounter. Show them the proper respect, or else they'll play even nastier tricks in the future!

COPPER DRAGON

As Trawli heard the whinny of a horse echo through the cave, she quietly cursed her luck. Moments later, Cantokrik the copper dragon's booming voice reverberated off the walls of the sun-drenched cavern.

"Look what I found! A horse that was tethered to a nearby tree. He was so quiet and obedient, patiently waiting for his master . . . but his smell gave him away . . ."

It was Broomback, Trawli's faithful steed, being held in the razor-sharp claws of a reptile that could swallow it in two ferocious bites.

"I smell you as well, tabaxi. Whiffs of cat dander and nervous sweat."

Trawli knew it was just a matter of time before the dragon found her hiding spot. Copper dragons were known for being playful, but also quite vindictive if the mood struck them.

"If you come on out and answer my riddle, I'll let you and your silly stallion be on your way. You can tell all your friends you survived meeting Cantokrik the Capricious."

Trawli knew there was a "but" coming . . .

"But if you don't . . . well then, I'll have a horse snack and be *very* annoyed!"

What should Trawli do? If she steps out and reveals herself, will Cantokrik keep his word or does he eat Broomback anyway? If the dragon asks Trawli a riddle, can she answer it correctly? Otherwise, if Trawli leaves her horse and tries to sneak away, will she be successful, or does the dragon track her down? Whatever happens next, it's up to you!

SILVER DRAGON

SPECIAL POWERS

COLD BREATH
Much like white dragons, their sworn enemies, these dragons can breathe a terrifying icy blast that can freeze a target solid or tear them apart with chunks of sharp ice.

PARALYZING BREATH
In addition to cold, silver dragons can exhale powerful energy that magically paralyzes everyone in its path, making their foes helpless targets.

Silver dragons are the kindest and most socially aware of all the metallic dragons. They feel a strong need to protect lesser races and assist good creatures in need.

These shimmering and noble reptiles enjoy the company of other humanoids and spend much of their time in humanoid form, building bonds with local townspeople or heroes without those mortals ever being aware of the silver dragon's true nature. They're fascinated by the short lives of many humanoids and their courage in the face of such mortality.

LAIR Silver dragons make their lairs on secluded mountain peaks and they prefer cold weather climates where possible. A natural cavern, a forgotten mine, or an abandoned mountaintop fortress are all ideal spots for a silver dragon to settle and raise a family.

DO THIS

Bring them historical items. Silver dragons are fascinated by humanoid history, especially from civilizations that no longer exist. Bring them something from a culture they haven't seen before and you may be able to gain their favor.

Appeal to their good nature. Silver dragons believe in justice for all creatures and instinctively want to protect the innocent. A compelling plea may sway them to aid you.

DON'T DO THIS

Don't expect them to stick around. Even if a silver dragon does help you, they go through long periods where they build their treasure hoards or raise their young. A silver dragon has a lifespan of hundreds of years, so they can easily lose track of time. Many mortals pass on before they get a chance to converse with the same silver dragon twice.

Don't command them. Silver dragons want to help, but that doesn't mean they're at your beck and call. These ancient creatures are powerful enough to destroy an entire city and make decisions for themselves.

GOLD DRAGON

💀 3-5

SPECIAL POWERS

FIRE BREATH
Much like red dragons, their sworn enemies, these dragons can breathe intense gouts of fire hot enough to melt metal, turning most non-magical equipment and armor into slag or smoldering ashes.

WEAKENING BREATH
In addition to fire, gold dragons can exhale powerful energy that magically weakens everyone in its path, making it hard for their foes to fight back against their majestic might.

Gold dragons are the most powerful and majestic of all the metallic dragon types. They are wise and strong, and they fervently battle against evil wherever it can be found.

Though they fight for the forces of light, gold dragons are also quite somber and aloof, preferring privacy to the kind of social interaction enjoyed by their silver cousins. A gold dragon in disguise as a humanoid or animal rarely reveals its true form, and they prefer to go about their plans in secret rather than work with others.

LAIR The secretive nature of gold dragons is also reflected in their choice of lair. These ancient protectors prefer extremely well-hidden homes tucked away in remote locations or deep underground. Mist-shrouded islands, ancient ruins in forgotten lands, or caves behind sparkling waterfalls are all possible places for gold dragons to build a secure lair.

A gold dragon's treasure hoard is a secret spot within their lair, usually guarded by powerful magical wards and traps.

DO THIS	DON'T DO THIS
Look for the mists. Shimmering mists tend to appear in regions where gold dragons have built a lair. It's a beautiful display and also a subtle hint that an area is under the dragon's protection.	**Don't try to surprise them.** Older gold dragons can see glimpses of the future, so it's almost impossible to sneak up or ambush them.
Gift them with wealth. Gold dragons can eat just about anything, but their preferred diet consists of gems and pearls. A large enough offering may gain their favor, if you absolutely need it.	**Don't expect them to be your ally.** Gold dragons are a positive force in the world, but they rarely team up with others, preferring to go about their virtuous tasks in secret. Leave them to their mission and know that it is being done for the greater good.

BAHAMUT, THE PLATINUM DRAGON

Bahamut is the legendary and majestic King of Good Dragons. He rarely makes his presence known in our world, but in times of great strife he may appear, especially if malevolent forces include Tiamat, the Queen of Evil Dragons, who is Bahamut's sworn enemy from across the ages.

A regular metallic dragon is one of the most awe-inspiring and intimidating creatures an adventurer could ever face, and Bahamut has the respect and reverence of all metallic dragons. Just being in his presence is enough to terrify the forces of evil or embolden armies of the just. Even still, only the most legendary heroes will ever glimpse Bahamut, let alone interact with the platinum dragon directly. Across dimensions and throughout worlds, he is worshipped and loved by good-aligned races and feared by the forces of darkness.

LAIR Bahamut lives in another dimension, called Mount Celestia, in a palace made entirely from the platinum dragon's treasure hoard. The walls of the palace are forged from mithral and the windows are composed of huge gemstones. Few mortals have ever seen Bahamut's palace and fewer still have stepped foot inside.

On our world, Bahamut will sometimes disguise himself as a venerable human peasant in simple robes. In this form, he is usually accompanied by seven golden canaries (seven ancient gold dragons who are also in disguise).

SPECIAL POWERS Bahamut has three different breath weapons available to him, although he can only use one at a time.

ICE BREATH
An incredibly cold blast of air that can extinguish fire, even dragon fire, and freeze anything in its path.

GASEOUS BREATH
A strange magical mist that briefly transforms anything it reaches into a gas as a way to keep allies from being hurt or to stop opponents from hurting others.

DISINTEGRATION BREATH
A devastating blue beam of light that fires out from Bahamut's mouth and destroys everything it touches.

SIZE Bahamut in his natural form is approximately sixty-feet long, which means he's one-third longer and taller than even the largest ancient metallic dragons. He's as long as a transport truck and almost twice as tall.

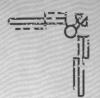

GARGANTUAN

Ogres are big. Dragons are huge. But some creatures are so enormous that they can devastate a city just by passing through it. Those are the creatures we call gargantuan. These titanic beasts can crush you without ever noticing you were there.

Purple worms have turned the tide of empires by eating an army, while rocs have plucked ancient temples off a hillside to use the wood for their nests. Yet even these creatures tremble in the presence of the terrible destructive power of the tarrasque.

Some monsters can really spoil your day. These gargantuan beasts can ruin a whole century! Are you ready to discover the biggest of the big?

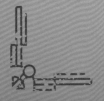

PURPLE WORM

SPECIAL POWERS

MOUTH
The giant maw of a purple worm can swallow a whole horse, so it can probably swallow you too.

STINGER
Unfortunately, you're no better off behind the worm. Its tail carries a giant stinger that can deliver a terrible attack filled with poison.

SIZE Purple worms can grow ten feet wide and up to eighty feet in length. That's longer than a bowling lane. In fact, a purple worm in a bowling lane could probably reach far enough to eat the person giving out the shoes!

Purple worms are among the most terrifying creatures in the Underdark. These giant, violet, writhing monsters are ravenous eaters, and they move at impressive speeds. Their huge teeth can chew through anything, including solid rock, but rock is not what they hunger for. Their favorite food is whatever squishy creatures they find underground, and that may include you!

Purple worms respond to vibrations and loud noises. They will follow these cues to devour whoever is responsible for the ruckus they detect. Sometimes a battle between two rival armies in the Underdark comes to a sudden and unexpected end when a purple worm bursts through a wall and swallows up warriors on both sides!

Purple worms rarely cover the same territory twice, so the tunnels they leave behind can become pathways for various races in the Underdark. Treasure hunters rush to fresh tunnels, because the undigestible things the worms leave behind may include precious metals and gemstones.

LAIR Purple worms never settle in one place; they spend their lives following vibrations in the earth and burrowing through rock in search of their next meal. However, don't assume you're safe aboveground. Purple worms have been sighted rising up through rocky terrain to swallow unsuspecting travelers.

DO THIS	DON'T DO THIS
Stay out of trouble. Worms follow noise, so keep away from crowds and battles.	**Don't let your guard down.** Purple worms move quickly, and when you're below the ground they can attack from any direction.
Look for places purple worms won't go. Worm tunnels are relatively safe. Established settlements in the Underdark often have magical wards to keep purple worms away.	**Don't hunt the worm.** Purple worms are often full of undigested treasures, which makes them a target for greedy hunters. The worms probably thought those hunters were very tasty.

ROC

SWIFT HUNTERS Rocs attack with their powerful beaks and their sharp talons. They fly at incredible speeds, and they see at great distances, which means they can swoop down on their prey with very little warning.

SIZE Rocs are so big that their outstretched wings measure about two hundred feet from tip to tip. That's the same wingspan as an international passenger jet. Their eggs are so tall that they could crush most adventurers.

Legend has it that rocs were created thousands of years ago when giants and dragons were waging war for control of the world. Dragons had a clear advantage, because they could attack the giants from above, so the giants used magic to create birds as big as dragons, which allowed them to bring the battle to the sky.

When the war was over, most rocs were released into the wild, where they spread their wings and sought out new homes wherever there was space and food enough for them to survive, though some larger and more powerful giants still keep rocs as pets.

Rocs are such large creatures that they need to hunt equally large prey, including whales, elephants, some dragons, and even the giants that once controlled them. To see a roc in the sky above you is an awesome and terrifying sight, but small creatures like you are usually beneath their notice.

LAIR Rocs are so huge that each one needs its own territory to hunt. They make their homes on the highest peaks of giant mountain ranges and build nests out of anything they can salvage, from wrecked ships to ruined buildings. Sometimes these ruins contain treasures, making roc nests a target for treasure hunters.

DO THIS

Keep calm. Even though a soaring roc can probably see you down on the ground with its excellent eyesight, it likely doesn't care about you.

Learn a feather fall spell. If you ever get caught up in a roc's talons and manage to break free, you'll find yourself a long way off the ground very quickly. Feather fall is a spell that can get you safely back down to earth.

DON'T DO THIS

Don't ride an elephant. At least, don't ride one if there's a roc overhead. You may be too small for a roc to hunt you, but an elephant is not.

Don't poke around its nest. A roc will not react kindly to anyone who ventures into its home or comes near its eggs.

TARRASQUE

EPIC

FRIGHTFUL PRESENCE An adventurer affected by this power is rooted to the spot, unable to approach or flee, which puts them at a big disadvantage. Anyone who successfully resists will be immune to this power for twenty-four hours.

SIZE A tarrasque is as tall as a five-story building and as long as two telephone poles laid end-to-end. It weighs as much as two blue whales, so you definitely don't want to be underneath when it decides to sit down.

The tarrasque may be the most dreaded monster anywhere. Its purpose and motivation is a mystery. No one knows where it lives or what prompts it to descend upon one place or another. The destruction left it in its wake is, however, indisputable.

Covered in thick scales and a rigid line of bony spikes, the beast's hide is tremendously difficult to pierce with melee or ranged weapons. This armored exterior repels most combat spells, sometimes turning the effect back on the caster. Its enormous jaw can swallow almost any creature whole, and it has been known to consume whole towns before departing.

It is widely believed that only a single tarrasque exists in all the realms. No one wants to be proven wrong about this.

LAIR The tarrasque has a secret lair deep within the earth, where it may slumber for decades or even centuries before rising to attack. There are few adventurers brave (or foolish) enough to go looking for it, and those who do are either unsuccessful—or never heard from again.

SWALLOW The only thing more unpleasant than being near a tarrasque is being inside one. Adventurers who have been swallowed must deal with darkness, limited space, and damage from the monster's potent stomach acid (*ewww*). By damaging the creature's innards, an adventurer may be able to force the tarrasque to vomit them up. That's pretty gross, but a lot less gross than being digested by a gigantic scaly monster.

DO THIS	DON'T DO THIS
Use magical weapons. Ordinary arms won't scratch a tarrasque's scaly surface.	**Don't get gobbled.** The inside of a tarrasque might be softer than the outside, but its nasty stomach acid makes being swallowed a bad idea.
Evacuate the innocent. You may not be able to stop the monster, so protect the people in its path by getting them to safety.	**Don't go solo.** Even the most legendary adventurers need allies to take on a tarrasque.

USING BEASTS
TO TELL YOUR OWN STORIES

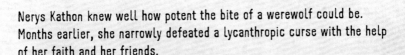

Nerys Kathon knew well how potent the bite of a werewolf could be. Months earlier, she narrowly defeated a lycanthropic curse with the help of her faith and her friends.

Now, standing in a chilly graveyard in the Fields of the Dead, she faced a werewolf again and her blood ran cold. Could she endure this horror *once more?*

The hulking beast snarled, a guttural pulsing sound echoing through the cold night air.

"You will never find the Silver Sigil, cleric of Kelemvor. Leave now or I'll rend your flesh with my claws."

Memories of sharp talons and even sharper teeth flooded back into Nerys's mind, but she knew she could not back down, not now. Too many lives hung in the balance if she failed.

With a sharp intake of breath, she gripped her sword tightly and charged.

Reading about beasts and battles ignites your imagination, doesn't it? Every profile, every illustration, begins to create little stories in your mind. What happened before that moment in time, what happens right after... it's all part of an exciting daydream that can't stay contained until you explore the possibilities.

All those wandering thoughts about action and adventure are the perfect way to begin building your own stories!

The ideas might start with a beast or behemoth, but they can go *anywhere*: the creature's lair, a sprawling city, tombs or dungeons, islands, caverns, or even underwater worlds. You get to choose all the ingredients that make up your story and then stir them together to make something new.

WHO IS YOUR MAIN CHARACTER?

- Are they like you or different? Young or old, human or something else?

WHERE DOES THE STORY TAKE PLACE?

- A mountain, a forest, underwater, or in a graveyard? Any of the locations in this book might inspire you, or you could create somewhere entirely different!

WHEN DOES THE STORY HAPPEN?

- At night or during the day, in the middle of a thunderstorm or right before the bells toll to ring in the new year? Combine ideas together and think about time passing as the story unfolds.

HOW DO THINGS CHANGE AS THE STORY CARRIES ON?

- Does the hero succeed or fail? Do they find somewhere new or explore somewhere old? Stories are about events, and events change us, so figure out what those changes are, and you'll see progression in your ideas.

WHAT SHOULD SOMEONE FEEL WHEN THEY READ YOUR STORY?

- Do you want them to laugh or get scared? Cheer or be grossed out? Knowing what your goals are can help when you're planning it all out.

Remember, you don't have to do it all on your own! It's fun to collaborate with other people and tell a story as a group. Each of you can contribute different parts and combine them to make something new and unexpected.

One person can set the scene by describing a fantastic place, then ask the others who they are in this story and what they want to do. Fill in the details together, bit by bit, and you'll be surprised at how the adventure grows and changes as it carries on.

WRITE a list of weird names and assign them to different characters and creatures.

DRAW a map of a fantasy land and make notes for each geographical feature and location.

DESIGN an insignia for the local kingdom and come up with a famous saying used by the people who live there.

These are all important exercises you can use to enhance your creativity. It's the exact same process that authors and designers use when they're coming up with the stories you read in books or comics, watch on TV or in the movies, or play in tabletop or video games. Every story you enjoy started with little ideas that turned into big ones and daydreams that grew into wondrous places we want to explore.

If you've read through all the creatures in this little monster manual and are looking for more DUNGEONS & DRAGONS material to ignite your imagination, the *Wizards & Spells* guide is packed with magical character classes and enchanted equipment to outfit your courageous adventurer. You know what dangers are out there, big or small, now figure out who your hero will be and *forge your future*!

All Rights Reserved.
Published in the United States by Ten Speed Press, an imprint of Random House, a division of Penguin Random House LLC, New York.
www.crownpublishing.com
www.tenspeed.com

Ten Speed Press and the Ten Speed Press colophon are registered trademarks of Penguin Random House LLC.

Library of Congress Cataloging-in-Publication Data

Names: Zub, Jim, author. | King, Stacy, author. | Wheeler, Andrew (Graphic
    novelist), author.
Title: Beasts & behemoths : a young adventurer's guide / Written By Jim Zub
    With Stacy King and Andrew Wheeler.
Other titles: Beasts and behemoths
Description: First edition. | California : Ten Speed Press, 2020. | Series:
    Dungeons & dragons young adventurer's guide | Audience: Ages 8-12
Identifiers: LCCN 2020004732 (print) | LCCN 2020004733 (ebook) |
    ISBN 9781984858788 (hardcover) | ISBN 9781984858795 (ebook)
Subjects: LCSH: Dungeons and dragons (Game)—Handbooks, manuals,
    etc.—Juvenile literature.
Classification: LCC GV1469.62.D84 Z83 2020 (print) | LCC GV1469.62.D84
    (ebook) | DDC 793.93—dc23
LC record available at https://lccn.loc.gov/2020004732
LC ebook record available at https://lccn.loc.gov/2020004733

Hardcover ISBN: 978-1-9848-5878-8
eBook ISBN: 978-1-9848-5879-5

Printed in China

Publisher: Aaron Wehner
Art Director and Designer: Betsy Stromberg
Editor: Shaida Boroumand
Managing Editor: Doug Ogan
Production Manager: Dan Myers
Wizards of the Coast Team: David Gershman, Kate Irwin, Adam Lee, Zoë Robinson, Hilary Ross, Liz Schuh
Illustrations: Conceptopolis, LLC

10 9 8 7 6 5 4 3 2

First Edition